Informing the legislative debate since 1914 _____

Guatemala: Political, Security, and Socio-Economic Conditions and U.S. Relations

Maureen Taft-Morales
Specialist in Latin American Affairs

August 7, 2014

Congressional Research Service

7-5700

www.crs.gov

R42580

Summary

Since the 1980s, Guatemala, the most populous country in Central America with a population of 15.5 million, has continued its transition from centuries of mostly autocratic rule toward representative government. A democratic constitution was adopted in 1985, and a democratically elected government was inaugurated in 1986. A violent 36-year civil war ended in 1996.

This report provides an overview of Guatemala's current political and economic conditions, relations with the United States, and several issues likely to figure in future decisions by Congress and the Administration regarding Guatemala. With respect to continued cooperation and foreign assistance, these issues include security and governance; protection of human rights and human rights conditions on some U.S. military aid to Guatemala; support for the International Commission against Impunity in Guatemala; combating narcotics trafficking and organized crime; trade relations; intercountry adoption; and unaccompanied children at the U.S. border.

President Otto Pérez Molina began his four-year term in January 2012. A former military commander who served during the civil war period, Pérez Molina faces concerns from some regarding his role in the human rights abuses committed during that period. In a landmark case, a Guatemalan court found former dictator Efrain Rios Montt guilty of genocide and crimes against humanity on May 10, 2013, but another court overturned his conviction days later. The trial is scheduled to resume in January 2015. Certain developments in 2014 have caused concern among some observers that there is a backlash against some of the judicial reforms that were achieved in recent years and that impunity for human rights violations and other crimes may rise again.

Guatemala continues to be plagued by security issues related to narcotics trafficking, the rise of organized crime, social inequality, and poverty. Upon taking office Pérez Molina announced a controversial position to decriminalize drugs as one policy initiative to address Guatemala's many problems. In his view, decriminalization has to be gradual, strongly regulated, and has to take place in the whole region, including producer and consumer countries. In the meantime, Pérez Molina vows to continue prosecuting and jailing drug-traffickers.

Economic growth was about 3.7% in 2013. Agriculture contributes about a fifth of Guatemala's GDP. According to the World Bank, Guatemala has one of the most unequal income distributions and highest levels of poverty in the hemisphere. Guatemala is part of the U.S.-Central America-Dominican Republic Free Trade Agreement (CAFTA-DR).

Relations between Guatemala and the United States have traditionally been close, but they have been strained at times by human rights and civil-military issues, long of interest to the U.S. Congress. U.S. policy objectives in Guatemala include strengthening democratic institutions; encouraging respect for human rights and the rule of law; supporting broad-based economic growth, sustainable development, and mutually beneficial trade relations; combating drug trafficking; supporting continued Central American integration, and addressing child migration.

Contents

Figures

Tables

Contacts

Political Situation

Guatemala has suffered much violence for decades. Currently, it is considered one of the most insecure countries in the world, with a rate of 34 homicides per 100,000 people, and 76% of the population expressing little or no trust in the police.[1] Guatemala endured a 36-year civil war, which ended in 1996 with the signing of peace accords. During most of that time the Guatemalan military was in power and engaged in violent repression against civil society organizations, and in gross violations of the human rights of its citizens, especially its majority indigenous population. Although Guatemala established a civilian democratic government in 1986, it took another 10 years to end the violence, during which time the military continued to engage in repression and violations of human rights. The United States maintained close relations with most Guatemalan governments before, during and after the civil war, including with the military governments.

Since the late 1980s, Guatemala has continued to consolidate its transition not only from decades of military rule, but also from a centuries-long tradition of mostly autocratic rule, toward representative government. Democratically elected civilian governments have governed Guatemala for 28 years now, making notable gains, such as carrying out significant military reforms and generally exerting effective control over the military. Nonetheless, democratic institutions remain fragile. In addition to military impunity for human rights violations and other crimes, drug trafficking, corruption, and grossly inequitable distribution of resources make political and social development difficult. Recent developments have caused concern among some observers that there is a backlash against some of the judicial reforms and that impunity for human rights violations and other crimes may rise again.

President Otto Pérez Molina

Former army general Otto Pérez Molina of the rightist Patriot Party (*Partido Patriota*, PP) was inaugurated as president of Guatemala in January 2012. He succeeded President Álvaro Colom of the center-left National Unity of Hope (*Unidad Nacional de Esperanza*, UNE) coalition. Pérez Molina is a controversial figure. He commanded army troops during the violent counterinsurgency campaign of the 1980s, was director of military intelligence during the 1990s, and has been linked by international human rights groups, the press, and others to human rights violations, including death squads and major political assassinations.[2] Pérez Molina is also known as a military moderate who opposed then-President Jorge Serrano's *autogolpe* (self-coup) in 1993, and was the military's negotiator for the Peace Accords that ended Guatemala's 36-year civil war in 1996. As a member of the Guatemalan Congress, he has advocated for legal and security reform, but has also been accused by the banking regulatory commission of involvement in the siphoning of state funds.[3] In 2011, U.S. citizen Jennifer Harbury filed the first step to

---

[1] Red de Seguridad y Defensa de América Latina (RESDAL), Public Security Index: Central America: Costa Rica, El Salvador, Guatemala, Honduras, Nicaragua, and Panama, Buenos Aires, October 2013, p. 66.

[2] See for example, Manuel Roig-Franzia, "Choosing a Future From Tainted Pasts: Both Presidential Candidates in Today's Vote in Guatemala Have Links to Some of the Nation's Most Painful Wounds," *Washington Post*, November 4, 2007, p. A18; Susan C. Peacock, Adriana Beltrán, *Hidden Powers in Post-Conflict Guatemala: Illegal Armed Groups and the Forces Behind Them*, Washington Office on Latin America, 2003, pp.19-20; Francisco Goldman, *The Art of Political Murder: Who Killed the Bishop?*, Grove Press, 2007, p. 385; and Tim Weiner, "Guatemalans Covered up Killing of an American, U.S. Aides Say," *New York Times*, March 24, 1996, p.1.

[3] Kate Joynes, "Accused Guatemalan Congress Chief Sidelined; Fiscal Reform Delayed," *Global Insight Daily* (continued...)

---

trigger an investigation of Pérez Molina for his alleged role in the 1992disappearance and murder of her husband, guerrilla leader Efrain Bámaca. Pérez Molina responded at the time that the case had gone nowhere before, and that the new effort had to be politically motivated.[4] During his campaign, Pérez Molina pledged to combat crime with a "mano dura," or iron fist, generally interpreted in Latin America to mean the use of repressive tactics. The party he created, the second-largest bloc in the previous legislature, generally opposed reforms proposed by the government under former President Colom, such as laws on rural development and the Law against the Illegal Accumulation of Wealth and Budget Expansion.[5]

The Perez Molina Administration

Since taking office in 2012, President Otto Pérez Molina has focused on reducing crime, increasing social spending, and enacting reforms to strengthen Guatemalan institutions. Early actions in support of judicial, social, and fiscal reform showed "surprisingly liberal inclinations," as one analyst put it.[6] Limited political will and resources, weak capacity, and a divided legislature have slowed progress in all those areas, however. President Pérez Molina, of the rightist Partido Patriota, vowed to strengthen the judicial system, and during the first half of his four-year term, progress was made toward that end. Then-Attorney General Claudia Paz y Paz, who had been appointed by his predecessor, pushed forward prominent human rights cases, reduced impunity for murder and other crimes, and improved the capacity of investigators and prosecutors. The U.N.-sponsored International Commission against Impunity in Guatemala (CICIG) supported those efforts, and proposed legislative reforms as well. In 2014, however, several events have indicated that vested interests are working to slow or reverse the judicial reforms accomplished in recent years.

The intimidation of judicial officials, widespread corruption, and the involvement of organized crime in violence and extortion are all widely seen as contributing to high levels of impunity and public mistrust in institutions. The Economist Intelligence Unit predicts that these characteristics, plus "a persistent failure of the state to provide basic public services to large parts of the population, ...will sustain the risk that public discontent results in widespread protest and social unrest in 2014-18."[7] Opposition to mining activities in rural areas, and the limited advances made in reducing Guatemala's high levels of poverty and inequitable distribution of wealth may also contribute to instability.

One high profile example of judicial intimidation and impunity involved the case of former dictator Efrain Rios Montt. Rios Montt was found guilty in May 2013 of genocide and crimes against humanity committed during his rule (1982 to 1983). Just days later, however, Guatemala's Constitutional Court overturned those verdicts, following pressure from the executive branch and from a powerful business association known as CACIF (the Spanish acronym for the

---

(...continued)

Analysis, June 18, 2008.

[4] "Jennifer Harbury Acciona Contra Pérez Molina," *Prensa Libre.com*, March 23, 2011, translation by author.

[5] International Crisis Group, *Guatemala's Elections: Clean Polls, Dirty Politics*, Policy Briefing, Latin America Briefing No. 24, Bogota/Brussels, June 16, 2011, p. 4.

[6] Robert Munks, "Further Civil War Abuse Trial Opens in Guatemala," *IHS Global Insight Daily Analysis*, March 14, 2012.

[7] Economist Intelligence Unit, *Country Report: Guatemala*, May 2014, p. 3.

Coordinating Committee of Agricultural, Commercial, Industrial, and Financial Associations).[8]
(See "Landmark Trial of Former Dictator Rios Montt" below.)

In April 2014 Guatemala's national bar association suspended Judge Yassmin Barrios from practicing law for one year. Barrios had overseen the Rios Montt trial, and has received international praise for her integrity and judicial independence. CICIG, the U.N. Office of the High Commissioner for Human Rights and various local and international human rights organizations have condemned the suspension.[9]

In May 2014, Attorney General Paz y Paz, who had pushed forward the Rios Montt case, among others, was forced to step down early after a judicial decision reduced her term based on a technicality. Paz y Paz, who began to pursue aggressively cases against former military officials while she served the Colom Administration, had continued to do so under the Pérez Molina Administration. In March 2012, a former Kaibil special forces officer was sentenced to over 6,000 years in prison for participating in the 1982 Dos Erres massacre of 201 men, women, and children. The Kaibiles, an elite special forces unit of the army, allegedly committed extensive human rights violations during Guatemala's civil war. Also in 2012, the government opened the trial of four former members of the Civil Self-Defense Patrols and a military commissioner, on charges of involvement in another 1982 massacre that killed 256 Mayan Guatemalans.[10]

CICIG and other international and local organizations criticized the nominating process for Attorney General as being nontransparent, noting that Paz y Paz had received the second highest grade among the initial pool of candidates, and had garnered international praise for her prosecutorial independence, yet was not included on the final list of candidates.

The President appointed Thelma Aldana as the new Attorney General, citing her 20 years of experience in the judicial branch, including as a Supreme Court Magistrate, and that she received the highest grade from the nominating commission evaluating candidates for the position. Attorney Lorena Escobar, an expert in security and justice with the Guatemalan Association of Research and Social Studies, described Aldana as a capable woman who would strengthen the fight against femicide; she also said that in order for Aldana to overcome the charges that she is linked to the executive branch and to the ruling party, Aldana "should give continuity to the investigations of crimes that occurred during the armed conflict and against ruling party mayors accused of corruption."[11] The President denied reports that Aldana had links to the ruling party, and said that international critics of the nominating process should not interfere in Guatemala's internal decisions.[12]

Human rights groups and other observers remain concerned that efforts to prosecute former military officials for human rights abuses face opposition from powerful elements in Guatemalan society. In May 2014, for example, the Guatemalan Congress passed a nonbinding resolution that

---

[8] El Periódico, "Gobierno señala injerencia internacional en sentencia por genocidio," May 15, 2013; and CACIF, "CACIF llama a Corte de Constitucionalidad a preservar gobernabilidad y futuro del país," press release, at http://www.cacif.org.gt, author's translations.

[9] Economist Intelligence Unit, *Country Report: Guatemala*, May 2014, pp. 27-28.

[10] Robert Munks, op. cit.

[11] Sergio Morales, Claudia Palma, "Thelma Aldana es la nueva Fiscal General," Prensa Libre.com, May 9, 2014.

[12] Sergio Morales, "Thelma Aldana es la nueva Fiscal General," video report at http://www.prensalibre.com/postuladora_fiscal_general/Preisente-nombrara-nuevo-fiscal-general_0_1135086685 html, May 9, 2014.

essentially denied that genocide occurred during Guatemala's civil war.[13] Proposed by a legislator from the Partido Republicano Institucional party, which was founded by Rios Montt (and called the Frente Republicano Guatemalteco at the time), the resolution stated that "the trial of the century" has "reopened polarization" in the country and impedes national reconciliation.

Human rights advocates and others also are wary that efforts might founder further under President Pérez Molina, who has repeatedly denied that the army committed genocide, and has come under increased scrutiny as a result of the Rios Montt trial.

Guatemala's next general elections are due to be held in late 2015. The Guatemalan constitution prohibits presidential reelection in a type of article known as "artículos pétreo," or articles set in stone, that explicitly cannot be reformed. Pérez Molina has generated controversy by calling for a constitutional reform to extend the presidential term to six years, and by inference, his own term, allowing him to remain in office for an additional two years.[14]

---

[13] A truth commission supported by the United Nations determined that state security forces were responsible for most of the 200,000 deaths during the civil war, and that violence targeted at the indigenous Mayan population amounted to genocide because the entire population was targeted. Text of the May 2014 resolution in Spanish provided by the Guatemalan Embassy.

[14] Economist Intelligence Unit, "Calls for Constitutional Reform Spark Controversy," June 6, 2014.

Figure 1. Map of Guatemala

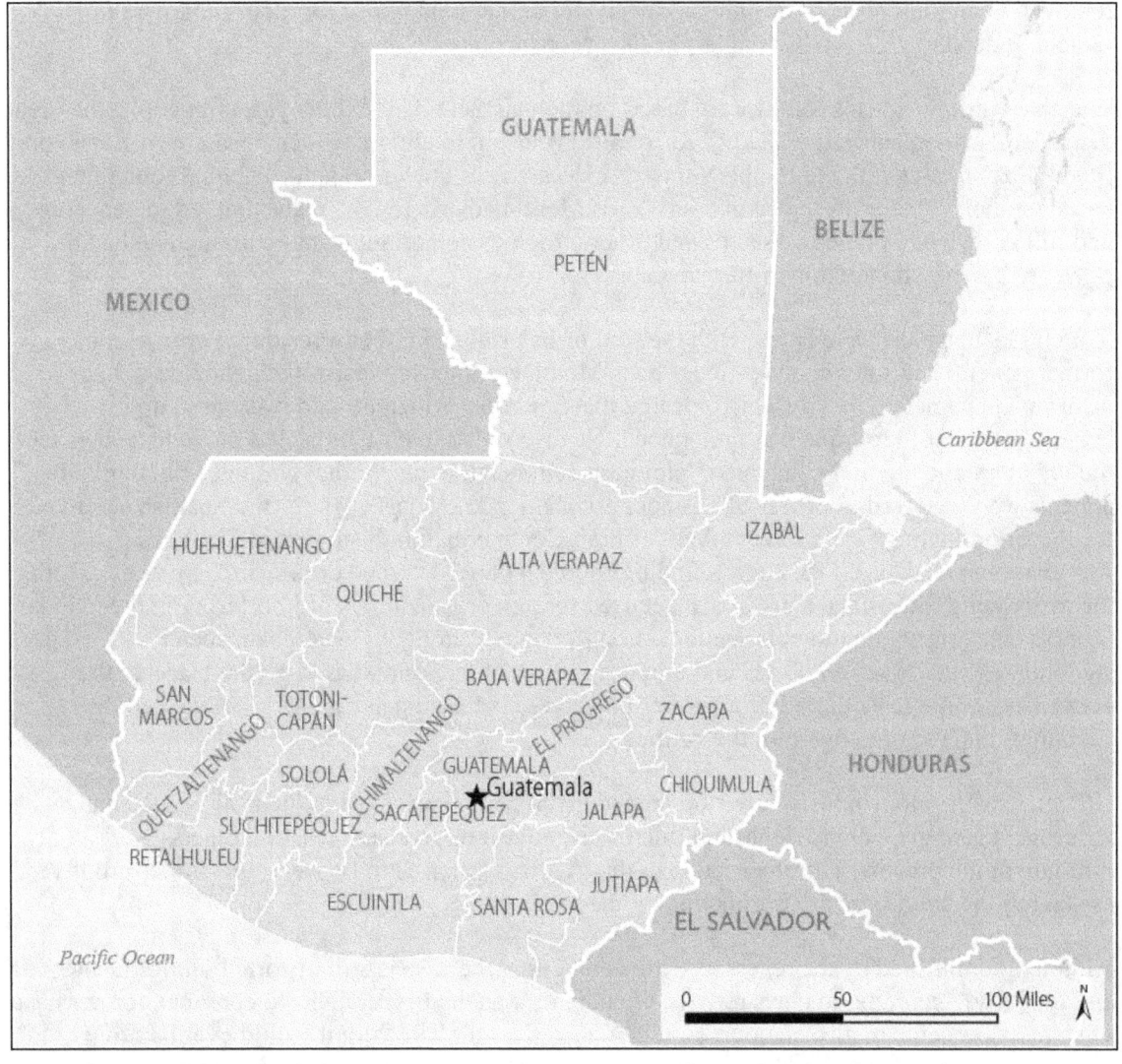

Source: CRS Graphics.

Landmark Trial of Former Dictator Rios Montt

On January 26, 2012—shortly after Pérez Molina took office—a Guatemalan judge ordered Efrain Rios Montt, dictator from the most violent civil war period from 1982 to 1983, to stand trial on charges of genocide and crimes against humanity. Within 16 months, on May 10, 2013, a Guatemalan court found the former general guilty on both charges. Rios Montt, who is 86 years old, was sentenced to 80 years in prison: 50 years for genocide and 30 years for crimes against humanity. He was sent directly from the courtroom to prison. Tried alongside him was his former head of military intelligence, Mauricio Rodriguez Sanchez. Rodriguez was acquitted of both charges; although he had written some of the military plans, the judges found that his command responsibility had not been proven.

Just 10 days later, however, Guatemala's Constitutional Court overturned those verdicts. The Guatemalan Public Ministry and civil parties challenged the ruling; the Center for Legal Action in Human Rights (CALDH) asked for the decision to be annulled. As discussed above, both the

Attorney General who brought the case to trial and the judge who oversaw the case have been removed from their positions. Both had received international praise for their integrity and judicial independence. A new trial has been set for January 2015.

The charges against Rios Montt were based on the massacre of 1,771 Mayan Ixil people, massive displacement, and subjecting the Ixil to conditions meant to eliminate them as a group. Survivors filed the complaint with the Public Ministry 13 years ago. The three-judge tribunal found that, based on the evidence presented in court, Rios Montt had ordered the plans that led to genocide, had full knowledge of the massacres and other atrocities committed, and—although he had the power to do so—did nothing to stop them.

Not all Guatemalans were happy with the trial or its original verdict. President Pérez Molina, a former general and a commander under Rios Montt, continues to insist that genocide did not occur in Guatemala. The President repeated that assertion, which he said was based on his experience, after the verdict was announced. He also stated that he respected the independence of the judiciary and the trial's judgment, although he noted that the verdict was not final until all appeals were resolved. A powerful business association known as CACIF (the Spanish acronym for the Coordinating Committee of Agricultural, Commercial, Industrial, and Financial Associations) challenged the court's findings and denounced "grave errors" in the process. Both the president's spokesman and CACIF accused foreign organizations of interfering in the judicial process and contributing to polarization among various sectors of Guatemalan society.[15] According to the *New York Times* and other reports, such pressure, based on the fear that the conviction would pave the way for further prosecutions for human rights violations, led the Constitutional Court to overturn the verdict.[16]

Others, usually anonymously, have threatened many people involved in the trial—Guatemalan judges and lawyers, human rights and rule of law advocates, researchers, and others—repeatedly throughout the process. The chief judge in the trial was reported to be wearing a bullet-proof vest as she left the courtroom after pronouncing the verdict.

Although diminished by the reversal of the conviction, the case is still historic both for Guatemala and globally. According to news reports, Guatemala was the first country to convict a former head of state of genocide in its own court system.[17] Few thought Rios Montt would ever be brought to trial, much less convicted, and hundreds of procedural delays and motions from the defense threatened to derail the process before the conviction was handed down. That the Guatemalan judicial system, still fragile and subject to corruption, was able to try a senior political leader, hold him responsible for gross human rights violations and international crimes, and have him serve any time at all was widely seen as a landmark victory for the rule of law. Human rights advocates also lauded the trial as a watershed moment for the indigenous population that was targeted during the war, saying it was the first time they were able to present their case in Guatemalan courts and receive a measure of justice for the human rights violations their community suffered.

---

[15] *ElPeriódico*, "Gobierno señala injerencia internacional en sentencia por genocidio," May 15, 2013; and CACIF, "CACIF llama a Corte de Constitucionalidad a preservar gobernabilidad y futuro del país," press release, at http://www.cacif.org.gt, author's translations.

[16] Elisabeth Malkin, "Guatemalan Court Overturns Genocide Conviction of Ex-Dictator," *New York Times*, May 20, 2013; Sonia Perez Diaz, "In Guatemala, Ex-Dictator Wins Genocide Decision," Pittsburgh Post- Gazette, May 22, 2013.

[17] Peru's judicial system convicted former President Alberto Fujimori of crimes against humanity in 2009.

Nonetheless, many human rights advocates believe that the overturning of Rios Montt's conviction again raises serious questions about the rule of law and the independence of the legal system in Guatemala, and, if allowed to stand, will reinforce impunity for current and former military officials.[18] A former Human Rights Ombudsman and president of the Constitutional Court concurred with the dissenting opinions of two sitting Constitutional Court judges, who said that the legal challenge was unfounded, and the majority's decision "improper," "disproportionate," and failed to take into account the rights of the victims.[19]

When meeting with President Pérez Molina in Guatemala on June 4, 2013, Secretary of State John Kerry congratulated the President "on the enormous progress that you have made with respect to your justice system, the strengthening of your justice system, the independence of that system."[20]

President Pérez Molina, who was a major in the army and a field commander under Rios Montt in the Ixil region at the time the massacres occurred, emerged more vulnerable after this trial. One witness, a former army officer, stated that Pérez Molina had participated in executions during the time in question. According to the *Wall Street Journal*, witnesses in other investigations have accused Pérez Molina of torture and executions as well.[21] Pérez Molina has denied the charges in the past. After delivering the verdict in the Rios Montt trial, chief judge Yassmin Barrios instructed prosecutors to continue investigations of others who may be responsible for those crimes. President Pérez Molina has immunity from prosecution through the end of his term in 2016. Some observers say that former U.S. officials who worked with the Rios Montt de facto government may also be vulnerable to charges emerging from investigations of those crimes.

Social Policies

Pérez Molina quickly created a Ministry of Social Development to implement social policy. By doing so, his Administration institutionalized social programs begun by earlier administrations and provided for greater coordination of the programs' operations. The ministry incorporated conditional cash transfer programs such as the "My Family Progresses" (*Mi Familia Progresa*) program created in 2008 as the cornerstone of former President Colom's antipoverty agenda. It included food pantries and cash payments of $40 per month for nearly 815,000 poor families to ensure children are in school and receive vaccines regularly.[22] Although those programs were popular, they were criticized for not being transparent enough; the establishment of a ministry is meant to address that issue.

According to the government, the Ministry's poverty reduction programs aim to break the intergenerational cycle of poverty by enhancing human development both in rural areas where

---

[18] See for example, Jo-Marie Burt, Geoff Thale, "The Guatemala Genocide Case: Using the Legal System to Defeat Justice," Washington Office on Latin America, June 5, 2013; and Emi MacLean, "Uncertainty Hovers over next Stages in Historic Guatemala Genocide Case after Constitutional Court Overturns Conviction," *The Trial of Efrain Rios Montt & Mauricio Rodriguez Sanchez,* Open Society Justice Initiative, May 28, 2013.

[19] Ibid.

[20] U.S. Department of State, "Secretary's Remarks: Remarks With Guatemalan President Otto Fernando Pérez Molina, June 4, 2013.

[21] Nicholas Casey, "World News: Guatemala Genocide Case Pressures Leader," *The Wall Street Journal*, May 13, 2013.

[22] Ezra Fieser, "Guatemala's Presidential Divorce of Convenience," *Christian Science Monitor*, June 17, 2011.

poverty is most severe and in urban areas.[23] Programs include conditional cash transfer programs that ensure children and adolescents stay in school and receive vaccines and other healthcare regularly; provision of food to vulnerable populations; and extracurricular skills-building activities for youth.

In 2012, then-U.S. Secretary of State Hillary Rodham Clinton praised "the quick work that President Pérez Molina in Guatemala has shown in creating a tax system aimed at beginning to collect taxes from the elites in that country."[24] Guatemala has one of the lowest tax collection rates in Latin America (11.2% of of gross domestic product (GDP) in 2011, according to the Department of State), and the private sector has fiercely resisted fiscal reform initiatives designed to provide the government with more resources to strengthen institutions and fight corruption. The two bills proposed by President Pérez Molina and passed by the legislature in 2012 are expected to provide 1.1% to 1.3% of GDP in additional revenue for social programs and improvements in security.[25]

The Guatemalan government announced a Pact for Security, Justice and Peace in late 2012, a strategy involving all state institutions to improve governability, security, and protection from crime, violence and impunity.[26] While the government has made progress in strengthening some institutions, widespread corruption and impunity continue to limit the extent to which reforms can be carried out and maintained.

Illicit Drug Policy

Perhaps most surprisingly for a politician who promotes an "iron fist" policy toward crime, President Pérez Molina has said since taking office in 2012 that the region needs to consider legalizing the use and transport of illicit drugs. Arguing that the United States has failed to curb illegal drug consumption, Pérez Molina has stated that his country has no choice but to seek alternatives to the current "war on drugs," in order to stem violence related to drug trafficking in Guatemala and in neighboring countries. U.S. officials oppose the idea, stating that drug legalization would not stop organized criminal elements from trafficking weapons and people.[27] The Guatemalan President has continued to push for legalization and regulation of drugs at international institutions such as the United Nations and the Organization of American States.

Land Use Conflicts

Land use continues to be a contentious issue during this administration. In March 2012 thousands of indigenous people marched over 120 miles to the capital to meet with President Pérez Molina and to demand the government settle land conflicts. The group that organized the march, the

---

[23] Gobierno de Guatemala, Ministerio de Desarrollo Social, http://www.mides.gob.gt/, accessed July 9, 2014.

[24] Federal Information & News Dispatach, Inc., *Remarks at the Transparency International-USA's Annual Integrity Award, State Dept. Press Releases and Documents*, Remarks, Hillary Rodham Clinton, Secretary of State, March 23, 2012.

[25] "Country Report: Guatemala," *Economist Intelligence Unit*, March 2012, pp. 3-5.

[26] Gobierno de Guatemala, Ministerio de Gobernación,
http://www.mingob.gob.gt/index.php?option=com_k2&view=item&layout=item&id=381&Itemid=563, accessed July 9, 2014.

[27] Romina Ruiz-Goiriena, "Guatemala President Weighs Drug Legalization, Blames US For Not Reducing Consumption," Associated Press, February 14, 2012.

Committee for Peasant Unity, said its principal demands included "an end to the evictions and criminal prosecution of Indians, a pardon for farm debts of more than … ($38.96 million) affecting more than 100,000 families, access to land and the end of mining in the region."

Mining issues are especially contentious, and often violent, throughout the region. Governments often see mines as a potential source of revenue for poverty reduction and social programs. Yet indigenous populations, which might be the beneficiaries of such programs, often object to mining under current conditions because they see it as violating their ancestral land rights, removing them from and/or damaging their source of livelihood, and/or excluding them from the decision making process as to how profits from mines in their communities should be spent.

In May 2013, President Pérez Molina declared a state of emergency in four southeastern towns after protests against a silver mine turned deadly. The Canadian-owned Escobal silver mine was given a final permit in April. Those opposing the mine say it will contaminate local water supplies. A series of conflicts began when security guards at the mine shot and wounded six protesters. The following day protesters kidnapped 23 police officers; when police went to free them, one police officer and a demonstrator were killed. The government at first said the state of emergency was related to violence at the mine, but later said it was linked to organized crime and the Los Zetas drug cartel. The state of emergency was lifted after eight days, then a state of alert went into effect for a brief period, which also limited some constitutional guarantees, such as the right of protest, and covered the town in which the mine is located.[28] According to the Guatemalan government, the mining company has signed an agreement with the former owners of the land on which it operates to give them 0.5% of the net earnings of commercial sales of the mine.[29] The former owners established a foundation that will invest 10% of those earnings in development projects in the surrounding communities. Guatemala says it is one of the first such agreements in Latin America.

Former Guatemalan First Lady Sandra Torres called on President Pérez Molina to suspend mining until related legal reforms are approved. Mining reforms currently being considered include higher royalty payments and greater social and environmental protections.[30] Torres, who was disqualified from running for President in the last elections (because of laws prohibiting relatives of sitting presidents from running), was reelected as general secretary of the UNE (National Unity of Hope) party in May 2013. Pérez Molina proposed a two-year stay on mining licenses; it is still pending in the Guatemalan Congress. Mining projects that have legally issued licenses have continued to operate.

Security Conditions

The focus of security issues in Guatemala has shifted from the violence of civil conflict to high levels of crime over the past quarter century. Weak institutions, remote areas with little effective state presence, and the country's geographic position between the drug producing nations of

---

[28] Sources for this paragraph include Business News Americas: "State of emegency not linked to anti-mining activity, Guatemala govt says," May 2, 2013, and "Guatemala govt lifts state of emergency in zone hit by anti-mining violence," May 10, 2013; and Reuters, "Guatemala declares emergency in 4 towns to quell mining protests," May 2, 2013.

[29] Email communication with Embassy of Guatemala official, Washington, DC.

[30] Business News Americas, "Guatemala: Politican [sic] demands mining moratorium pending reforms, press report," May 13, 2013.

South America and consumers in the United States have made Guatemala a prime target for drug traffickers and other organized criminal groups. Crime and violence have been extremely high in recent years, and officials estimated that up to 60% of Guatemalan territory may be under the effective control of drug traffickers.[31] The Guatemalan government has made some progress in addressing crime and impunity, with the help of the U.N.-supported Commission Against Impunity in Guatemala (CICIG). The country's fragmented political system, inconsistent political will, and weak judicial and security institutions remain serious obstacles to addressing the problem adequately.

In addition, Guatemala's widespread poverty and high levels of inequality and unemployment make much of its population especially vulnerable to crime. Almost one in four (23.3%) Guatemalan respondents in a 2010 survey reported being the victim of a crime in the previous year, ranking Guatemala only behind El Salvador among the Central American nations. The rate of homicides in Guatemala in 2010 was about 41 per 100,000 inhabitants, placing Guatemala in the middle of the region, at fourth of seven. Though still relatively high, the 2010 homicide rate was the lowest it had been since 2005.[32] In 2012 the national homicide rate dropped to 39.9 per 100,000. Preliminary figures for 2013, however, showed homicide rates rising again in 15 of Guatemala's 22 departments.[33]

Some crime is attributed to youth gangs, ranging from localized groups to national groups with international ties, including to gangs in the United States. The regions within Guatemala evidencing the highest murder rates, however, tend to be those where organized criminal groups and drug traffickers, not gangs, are most active.[34]

Involvement of the Military in Internal Security

In response to the high level of violence, a number of municipalities have asked for military troops to augment their ineffective police forces; the Guatemalan government, as under the previous four administrations, is using a constitutional clause to have the army "temporarily" support the police in combating rising crime. The day following his inauguration, President Pérez Molina stated, "Today, publicly, I want to lay out for the army an important goal of collaborating, coordinating and cooperating with other security institutions, and that is to put an end to the external threats and contribute to neutralizing illegal armed groups by means of military power."[35]

Despite efforts to develop a comprehensive, whole-of-government approach to security, successive governments' actions have often been reactive and dependent on the military. Human rights groups and other analysts have warned against militarization of law enforcement, noting

---

[31] "Drug Traffickers Have Stranglehold on Guatemala Says Top Prosecutor," *El País*, February 23, 2011.

[32] Crime victimization rates from Americas Barometer survey data from 2010 by the Latin American Public Opinion Project of Vanderbilt University; homicide rates from U.N. Office on Drugs and Crime; for tables and further information, see CRS Report R41731, *Central America Regional Security Initiative: Background and Policy Issues for Congress*, by Peter J. Meyer and Clare Ribando Seelke (data on pp. 4-5).

[33] RESDAL, *Public Security Index, Central America: Costa Rica/El Salvador/Guatemala,/ Honduras/Nicaragua/ Panama*, 2013, p. 67.

[34] Reports by Washington Office on Latin America and Instituto Tecnologico Autonomo de Mexico, and UNODC, as cited in CRS Report RL34112, *Gangs in Central America*, by Clare Ribando Seelke, p. 5.

[35] CNN Wire Staff, "Guatemala's President Calls on Troops to 'Neutralize' Organized Crime," *CNN.com*, January 16, 2012.

the peace accords' call for the army to focus solely on external threats, "the government's failure to investigate and punish unlawful killings committed by members of the security forces,"[36] and now, Pérez Molina's high rank in the military during the civil war.

In 2012 Mayan citizens were protesting high electricity prices and demanding affordable education and the recognition of indigenous rights when Guatemalan soldiers shot at the crowd, killing six people and injuring another thirty. After initially denying military responsibility for the violence, President Pérez Molina then allowed for a thorough investigation, and soldiers were prosecuted for their role.

While in recent years observers said the executive branch appeared to exhibit effective control over the military, the State Department's 2013 human rights report noted that civilian authorities "on occasion" failed to exert such control.

Guatemalan Cooperation with CICIG

Beginning in 2008, Guatemalan judicial officials worked with CICIG (see section on "International Commission against Impunity in Guatemala" below) to investigate and prosecute illegal groups and clandestine structures, including some through which many former and current military officers allegedly engage in human rights violations, drug trafficking, and organized crime.

> ... [CICIG] has spurred a series of criminal investigations compromising some of the country's most powerful figures—despite occasional setbacks. A new head of the national prosecution service has managed to shape an extraordinary turnaround, ordering the arrest of several 'untouchable' druglords, as well as a former president and general accused of atrocities during the civil war. Drug interdictions have soared; the murder rate has fallen, albeit slightly; even impunity rates for serious crimes are down.
>
> This progress cannot hide the dilapidation of the country's security and justice institutions, ... nor the acute fear of crime that is felt by many Guatemalans. But in combination with the Central American region's determination to address its vulnerabilities to transnational crime, it does offer some reason to believe that the crisis may be contained.[37]

Others acknowledged the accomplishments, but expressed serious reservations. CICIG's former director, Francisco Dall'Anese, noted that CICIG can "build up the state, and create the legal conditions for the thing to function. Everything else depends on the willingness of the Guatemalans.... if you end up with the best system in Latin America and it is not used properly or is used for other purposes, there has been no progress."[38]

---

[36] U.S. Department of State, Bureau of Democracy, Human Rights, and Labor, *2010 Human Rights Reports: Guatemala*, 2010 Country Reports on Human Rights Practices, April 8, 2011, p. 1, http://www.state.gov/j/drl/rls/hrrpt/2010/wha/154507 htm.

[37] Ivan Briscoe and Marlies Stappers, *Breaking the Wave: Critical Steps in the Fight against Crime in Guatemala*, Clingendael Institute, Impunity Watch, January 2012, p. 3.

[38] Daniel Pacheco, *Guatemala Must Fight Impunity from Within: CICIG Director*, In Sight: Organized Crime in the Americas, June 1, 2012, http://www.insightcrime.org/insight-latest-news/item/2711-guatemala-must-fight-impunity-from-within-cicig-director.

After the reversal of Rios Montt's conviction, the early termination of Paz y Paz's term, other apparent reactions against efforts to hold military and other officials accountable, and President Pérez Molina's decision not to renew CICIG's mandate, the Economist warned in May 2014 that "there are lingering risks that impunity levels will worsen again."

Regional Security Efforts

Guatemala is part of Central America's "Northern Triangle" region, along with El Salvador and Honduras. These countries have all felt the impact of the Mexican government's campaign against drug-trafficking organizations, as some of those organizations move their operations into their territory and operate across borders. In response, the Northern Triangle countries have generally adopted aggressive tactics, supplanting their weak police forces with military forces. Dall'Anese, a former attorney general of Costa Rica, also noted the limited resources of Guatemala and the other Central American nations: "Very often the budget of a country in Central America … is less than the petty cash fund of a criminal organization."[39] One way to address the inequity of resources, he suggested, might be to create regional courts, to share resources and capacity. These and other ideas are being explored by Guatemala and its neighbors as they seek to improve regional efforts. They have various organizations through which they address security, such as the Central American Integration System (known by its Spanish acronym, SICA) and the Central American Armed Forces Conference (CFAC, to which only El Salvador, Guatemala, Honduras, and Nicaragua, plus the Dominican Republic, belong, but not Belize, Costa Rica, or Panama). Translating theoretical agreement on the need to cooperate on security matters into an operational institutional framework has proved difficult, however, in the face of differing priorities and approaches, and border and other types of disputes within the region.[40]

Economic and Social Conditions

Guatemala has the biggest economy in Central America, yet ranks lowest in that region, and 133rd out of 187 countries on the Human Development Index for 2013. With a 2013 gross domestic product (GDP) of $54 billion and a per capita income of $3,341, Guatemala is considered a lower middle income developing economy by the World Bank.[41]

The country has maintained generally sound macroeconomic policies, and enjoyed annual GDP growth rates of over 5% before the economy slowed as a result of the onset of the global financial crisis and U.S. recession. Significant declines in exports, remittances, and foreign direct investment slowed growth to 0.6% in 2009. The Guatemalan economy began to recover in 2010, with GDP growth of 2.9%, although a series of natural disasters in 2010 and 2011 caused losses and damages estimated at almost $2 billion. The recovery has continued, with economic growth estimated at 3.3% for 2013, and forecast to be 3.4% in 2014.[42] Guatemala's top exports are knit apparel, edible fruit and nuts, precious stones (gold), spices, coffee and tea, and woven apparel.[43]

---

[39] Ibid.

[40] Latin American Newsletters, "Central America: Prospects for a New US-backed Regional Scheme," *Latin American Security & Strategic Review*, no. SSR-11-02 (February 2011).

[41] World Bank data online, at http://data.worldbank.org/country/guatemala, accessed July 29, 2014.

[42] Data in this paragraph and the next from: World Bank, "Guatemala Overview," April 9, 2014.

[43] Office of the U.S. Trade Representative, *Guatemala: U.S.-Guatemala Trade Facts*, http://www.ustr.gov/countries-
(continued...)

Despite improvements in political and macroeconomic stability, Guatemala's levels of poverty and inequality remain among the highest in the region. According to the World Bank, although Guatemala reduced poverty by five points between 2000 and 2006, from 56% to 51%, the percent of the population living in poverty rose again to just under 54% by 2011.

Guatemala's income distribution is one of the most unequal in the world, and has gotten worse. In 2002 the wealthiest 10% of Guatemalans consumed over 42% of Guatemala's total income, while the poorest 10% accounted for just 1.4%. In the latest figures, the wealthiest 10% consume over 47% of Guatemala's total income, while the poorest 10% account for just 1% of the total national income.[44]

Guatemala's social development indicators often fall below those of countries with lower per capita incomes.[45] The maternal mortality rate is 120 per 100,000; the infant mortality rate is 25 per 1,000, amongst the highest in Latin America.[46] Chronic child malnutrition is at about 50%, the highest rate in Latin America, and fourth-highest rate in the world.[47] The proportion of the population living with hunger has increased by 80% over the past 20 years, from about 17% in 1991, to 30.5% in 2012.[48] This economic and social marginalization disproportionately affects Guatemala's indigenous population. Indigenous peoples comprise 24 different ethno-linguistic groups and account for roughly half of Guatemala's 15.5 million people. Over 42% of the rural population, which is mostly indigenous, lives in extreme poverty, compared to 29% nationally.[49] Child malnutrition among the indigenous is almost 70%.[50]

U.S. Relations With and Aid to Guatemala

Relations between the United States and Guatemala traditionally have been close, but there has been friction at times over human rights and civil/military issues. According to the Department of State, U.S. policy objectives in Guatemala include supporting the institutionalization of democracy and implementation of the peace accords; encouraging respect for human rights and rule of law, and the efficient functioning of the International Commission against Impunity in Guatemala (CICIG); supporting broad-based economic growth and sustainable development and sustainable development; cooperating to fight money laundering, corruption, narcotics trafficking, trafficking in persons, and other transnational crimes; and supporting Central American integration through support for resolution of border and territorial disputes.[51]

(...continued)

regions/americas/guatemala, April 29, 2014, accessed July 25, 2014.

[44] U.N. Economic Commission for Latin America and the Caribbean (ECLAC), *Statistical Yearbook for Latin America and the Caribbean, 2013*, December 2013, p. 78.

[45] U.S. Department of State, "Background Note: Guatemala," March 22, 2010.

[46] United Nations Development Programme, *Human Development Report 2013*, 2013, pp. 158,168.

[47] World Food Programme, *Guatemala,* at http://www.wfp.org/countries/Guatemala/Overview, accessed July 29, 2014.

[48] United Nations, Millennium Development Goals Indicators, "MDG Country Progress Snapshot: Guatemala," http://mdgs.un.org/unsd/mdg/Resources/Static/Products/Progress2013/Snapshots/GTM.pdf.

[49] ECLAC, op. cit., p. 75.

[50] World Food Programme, op. cit.

[51] U.S. Department of State, "U.S. Relations with Guatemala," Fact Sheet, August 23, 2013.

Guatemala and the United States have significant trade relations. They are part of the Dominican Republic-Central America-United States Free Trade Agreement (CAFTA-DR), which began to be implemented in 2006. Supporters of CAFTA-DR point to reforms it spurred in transparency, customs administration, intellectual property rights, and government regulation. Critics note that the commercial balance between the two countries previously favored Guatemala, and the balance has shifted in favor of the United States, with Guatemala registering its first trade deficit in a decade after CAFTA-DR was signed.

Top priorities for U.S. bilateral assistance to Guatemala are addressing security and justice for citizens; improving food security and reducing chronic malnutrition; providing access to health services, promoting better educational outcomes; and managing natural resources to mitigate the impact of global climate change.[52] Various programs are integrated for a greater impact in the Western Highlands, which has the highest rates of poverty and chronic malnutrition in the country.

Table 1. U.S. Assistance to Guatemala by Account and Fiscal Year

($ in thousands)	Fiscal Year			
	2013 Actual	2014 Estimate	2015 Request	Increase / Decrease
TOTAL	80,779	65, 249	77,107	11,858
Development Assistance	45, 861	42, 789	57,387	14,598
Foreign Military Financing	712	1,740	1,000	-740
Global Health Programs- USAID	16, 796	15,000	13,000	-2000
International Military Education and Training	688	720	720	-
International Narcotics Control and Law Enforcement	4,846	-	-	-
P.L. 480 Title II	11,876	5,000	5,000	-

Source: Congressional Budget Justification, Foreign Operations, Fiscal Year 2013

The United States also provides assistance to Guatemala through two regional initiatives, the Central American Regional Security Initiative (CARSI) -for combating narcotics trafficking and preventing transnational crime-and the President's Emergency Plan for AIDS Relief (PEPFAR). According to the State Department, "The goal of all U.S. assistance efforts is to create effective structures and organizations that can be sustained by the Government of Guatemala."

The Administration's FY2015 request for aid to Guatemala totals $77 million, an overall increase of almost $12 million from FY2014 funding (see **Table 1**). It includes approximately $57 million for Development Assistance; $1 million for Foreign Military Financing (FMF); $13 million for Global Health Programs (U.S. Agency for International Development); $720,000 for International Military Education and Training (IMET); and $5 million for food aid (P.L. 480 Title II).

---

[52] U.S. Department of State, *Congressional Budget Justification: Foreign Operations, Fiscal Year 2015*, Appendix 3: Regional Perspectives. The section on aid to Guatemala is on pp. 658-663, and is drawn on for this section.

Congressional Concerns

Protection of Human Rights and Conditions on U.S. Military Aid

During most of Guatemala's 36-year civil war, the Guatemalan military was in power and engaged in violent repression against civil society organizations, and in gross violations of the human rights of its citizens, especially its majority indigenous population. Although Guatemala established a civilian democratic government in 1986, it took another 10 years to end the violence, during which time the military continued to engage in repression and violations of human rights. Civilians have governed Guatemala for about 28 years now, making notable gains, such as carrying out significant military and police reforms. Nonetheless, democratic institutions remain fragile, and security forces continue to enjoy widespread impunity for human rights and other crimes.

The U.S. State Department's most recent human rights report on Guatemala said that civilian authorities sometimes failed to maintain effective control over security forces, which commit human rights abuses. The report also said that:

> Principal human rights abuses included widespread institutional corruption, particularly in the police and judicial sectors; police and military involvement in serious crimes such as kidnapping, drug trafficking, and extortion; and societal violence, including often lethal violence, against women.

> Other human rights problems also included abuse and mistreatment by National Civil Police (PNC) members; harsh and life-threatening prison conditions; arbitrary arrest and detention; prolonged pretrial detention; failure of the judicial system to ensure full and timely investigations and fair trials; and failure to protect judicial officials, witnesses, and civil society representatives from intimidation and threats. There were also killings of journalists and trade unionists; sexual harassment and discrimination against women; child abuse, including commercial sexual exploitation of children; discrimination and abuse of persons with disabilities; and trafficking in persons. Other problems included marginalization of indigenous communities and ineffective demarcation of their lands; discrimination on the basis of sexual orientation and gender identity; and ineffective enforcement of labor and child labor laws.[53]

The international community is continuing to combat military impunity for human rights violations and other crime through support of the International Commission against Impunity in Guatemala (CICIG), rule of law, judicial and police reform, and other types of democracy-strengthening programs. Under former Attorney General Claudia Paz y Paz (2010- May 2014), the Public Ministry worked in conjunction with CICIG, and prosecuted officials who committed abuses and fraud. Paz y Paz, who had prosecuted extremely difficult cases such as the Rios Montt case, was forced to step down several months early on a technicality. Pérez Molina appointed a new Attorney General, Magistrate Thelma Aldana, in May 2014.

The U.N. High Commissioner for Human Rights visited Guatemala in March 2012. Commissioner Navi Pillay commended Guatemala for the direction it was taking to address

---

[53] U.S. Department of State, Bureau of Democracy, Human Rights, and Labor, *Country Reports on Human Rights Practices for 2013*, "Guatemala," 2014, p. 1.

"staggering impunity," including, since 2010, the first successful prosecution of cases for past human rights violations, and the ratification of the Rome Statute, the treaty establishing the International Criminal Court.[54] She also stated that the government must operate within the framework of the Peace Accords, the rule of law, and respect for the human rights of all Guatemalans as it attacks the country's high levels of insecurity, crime, and violence. Although indigenous people constitute the majority of the population, she said, they continue to be subject to social and economic exclusion and denial of their human rights. The U.N. official expressed particular concern over the negative impact of economic investment projects on the rights of indigenous peoples.

In 2011, a Guatemalan court sentenced four former soldiers to over 6,000 years each in prison for a 1982 massacre of hundreds of civilians and crimes against humanity during the country's civil war.[55] This was only the second time a trial was held in Guatemala relating to a civil war massacre. In 2012, Guatemala became the first country to find a former head of state guilty of genocide when it convicted Rios Montt for human rights crimes committed during the civil war. (See "Landmark Trial of Former Dictator Rios Montt" above.) His conviction was overturned 10 days later, which many observers saw as a major setback for the rule of law in Guatemala.

Guatemala had acquitted another former head of state, on embezzlement charges, in 2011. The United States filed separate charges against former President Alfonso Portillo (2000-2004) for conspiring to launder $70 million in state funds through U.S. banks. In May, 2013, Guatemala extradited Portillo to the United States to face corruption charges. Portillo pled guilty to conspiring to launder $2.5 million in March 2014.

Conditions on U.S. Military Aid to Guatemala

In 1990, President George H. W. Bush suspended overt military aid to Guatemala because of concerns over human rights abuses allegedly committed by Guatemalan security forces. In 2005, the United States began to allow Foreign Military Sales to Guatemala in recognition of progress the Guatemalan government had made in reforming the military.[56] Since 2008, Congress has allowed Foreign Military Financing (FMF) and International Military Education and Training (IMET) to Guatemala, but only to certain components of the armed forces, and with human rights conditions attached in the foreign assistance appropriations acts.

Congress placed conditions on aid to Guatemala in the FY2014 Consolidated Appropriations Act (P.L. 113-76), stating that assistance for the Guatemalan army may only be made available if the Secretary of State certifies that the Guatemalan government is taking credible steps to implement the 2010 Reparations Plan for Damages Suffered by the Communities Affected by the Construction of the Chixoy Hydroelectric Dam. The law also stated that no IMET or FMF funds may be expended for assistance for the Guatemalan Armed Forces until the Secretary of State certifies to the Committees on Appropriations that the Guatemalan government has resolved all cases involving Guatemalan children and American adoptive parents pending since December 31, 2007, or that it is making significant progress toward meeting a specific time-table for resolving

---

[54] "Guatemala Must Address Rule Of Law Challenges: UN," *India Blooms News Service*, March 17, 2012.

[55] Ken Ellingwood, "Rights Groups Praise Troops' Trials; Guatemala Convicts Four Ex-Soldiers in a 1982 Massacre during the Brutal Civil War," *Los Angeles Times*, August 4, 2011.

[56] Ibid; John Hendren, "Guatemala Gets U.S. Military Aid; A 15-Year Freeze on the Funds because of Human Rights Abuses is Lifted in Recognition of Reforms," *Los Angeles Times*, March 25, 2005.

those cases. Those conditions apply to aid provided through the Foreign Operations appropriations act, but not to aid provided through the Department of Defense (DOD). Most DOD aid goes through regional programs, so it is always difficult to get precise amounts for aid to any one country.

The Pérez Molina Administration, like previous Guatemalan governments, has been pressing the United States to drop those conditions and provide increased military aid to the army. The Obama Administration's request for foreign aid for FY2015 includes proposed funding for the Guatemalan army (see **Table 1**). According to the Administration's budget request, the FMF would "enhance the capacity of the Guatemalan military to secure national territory", provide maritime security against transnational threats, and support humanitarian aid operations. IMET proposed for FY2015 would "support professionalization training for the Guatemalan military," and provide training in democratic values and respect for human rights and in technical areas such as aircraft maintenance.

According to the State Department's human rights report, civilian authorities sometimes failed to maintain effective control over the security forces. It also reported that members of both the military and the police committed human rights abuses, and that "the level of impunity for security forces accused of committing crimes was high." Human rights advocates and others say that the Constitutional Court's decision to overturn Rios Montt's conviction, if it stands, would show that the military still enjoys impunity for human rights and other crimes.

The Department of Defense provides military assistance, mostly for counternarcotics programs, some of which is not subject to the human rights conditions described above, as it is authorized through the defense appropriations, rather than through the foreign assistance appropriations acts. DOD military assistance to Guatemala is subject to requirements for vetting participants to exclude those with records of human rights violations. These are known as Leahy conditions, after the Senator who incorporated them into legislation.[57] In FY2009-FY2010, the Department of Defense spent $3.5 million on counternarcotics operations centers in Guatemala, including $754,000 for a base for the Guatemalan army's *Kaibil* special forces.[58] As mentioned above, the Kaibiles are alleged to have committed extensive human rights violations during Guatemala's civil war. In addition, many ex-Kaibiles are reported to be members of the Mexican Los Zetas criminal organization. Four former Kaibiles were sentenced in 2011, another in March 2012, and another 12 remain fugitives from justice, for their roles in the 1982 Dos Erres massacre.

International Commission against Impunity in Guatemala

The United States and other donors support the International Commission against Impunity in Guatemala (CICIG), which was created in 2007 under the auspices of the United Nations. The commission's mandate is to help Guatemala dismantle illegal groups and clandestine structures responsible for organized crime, human rights violations, and other crimes through investigations and prosecutions. After its first year of operation, CICIG noted that the Guatemalan government

---

[57] For more on the Leahy laws, please see CRS Report R43361, *"Leahy Law" Human Rights Provisions and Security Assistance: Issue Overview*, coordinated by Nina M. Serafino.

[58] Michael Vickers, Asst. Sec. of Defense, *FY2009 Section 1022(a) Report*, Department of Defense, Letter to Hon. Ike Skelton, Chairman, Committee on Armed Services, February 17, 2010, p. 25, and Michele Flournoy, Under Sec. of Defense, *Fiscal Year 2010 DoD Foreign Counterdrug Activity Report*, Department of Defense, Letter to Hon. Carl Levin, Chairman, Committee on Armed Services, April 4, 2011, p. 7.

faced enormous challenges, but had begun to clean up the security forces and strengthen civil institutions.[59] Since then, CICIG has helped Guatemala investigate and prosecute important cases; a number of former high-level officials have been charged with corruption, faced trials, and been convicted. In 2013, the CICIG-vetted prosecutors unit in the Guatemalan Public Ministry achieved convictions in the trials of a former chief of criminal investigations of the Guatemalan National Civil Police (PNC) and two former police investigators for the extrajudicial killing of ten inmates between 2005 and 2006; and of a former police chief, former PNC chief of antinarcotics, and former PNC officer for drug trafficking.[60] All received sentences of significant time in prison.

CICIG has helped prevent a number of individuals with significant ties to corruption and/or organized crime from being appointed to senior positions in the Guatemalan state, and the Guatemalan government has approved CICIG-recommended legislative reforms.[61]

Nonetheless, CICIG and reform-minded elements of the government reportedly continue to be thwarted regularly by vested interests such as corrupt law enforcement and other public officials with alleged ties to criminal organizations. CICIG helped the Guatemalan judicial system to extradite, investigate, and prosecute former President Alfonso Portillo (2000-2004) for allegedly embezzling $15 million in government funds, only to have a panel of judges dismiss the charges this past May with reasoning that CICIG said was "neither valid nor logical."[62] Cases such as this demonstrate both the progress that has been made with CICIG's assistance, and the obstacles to reform still remaining. (Guatemala did extradite Portillo to the United States in May 2013, however, where pled guilty in March 2014 to bribery.)

President Pérez Molina has said that he will not extend CICIG's term when it expires in 2015. In its Sixth Report, CICIG wrote, "In order for the [Guatemalan] State to be sufficiently coordinated to tackle criminal organizations without CICIG support, a steely commitment and political intent will be necessary on the part of the institutions so as to implement the recommendations made since August 2010..."

Illicit Narcotics Trafficking and Other Organized Crime[63]

In recent years Congress has become increasingly concerned over the increase in drug trafficking-related violence across Central America. It first appropriated higher levels of assistance for these countries to combat organized crime and drug trafficking through the Mérida Initiative, created mostly to help Mexico, then, beginning in FY2010, through the Central America Regional Security Initiative (CARSI).

---

[59] International Commission against Impunity in Guatemala, *One Year Later,* September 2008, Guatemala, available at http://www.cicig.org/Publications html.

[60] U.S. Department of State, Bureau of Democracy, Human Rights, and Labor, *Country Reports on Human Rights Practices for 2013 "Guatemala,"* 2014, p. 3.

[61] Comisión Internacional Contra la Impunidad en Guatemala (CICIG), *Tercer Año de Labores*, September 2010.

[62] CICIG, "Apela Sentencia Absolutoria del ex Presidente Portillo y Dos ex Ministros," press release no. 041, May 30, 2011, translation by author; and "Impunity in Guatemala: Two Steps Forward, One Step Back," *Economist*, June 8, 2011.

[63] Information in this section drawn from U.S. Department of State: *2013 International Narcotics Control Strategy Report: Guatemala*, volume I, Drug and Chemical Control, and volume II, Money Laundering and Financial Crimes, March 5, 2013, and *Money Laundering and Financial Crimes Country Database: Guatemala*, May 2011.

The end of Guatemala's civil war roughly coincided with the spread of drug trafficking rings throughout Central America. Many former combatants shifted into drug trafficking and other organized crime. A weak judicial system, with inadequate enforcement of laws and widespread impunity, has fostered the growth of widespread corruption and high levels of criminal activities in Guatemala. Partly as a consequence of having one of the lowest tax collection rates in Latin America, and a private sector that resists fiscal reform, the Guatemalan government has been unable to dedicate adequate resources to strengthening judicial institutions and fighting corruption. Furthermore, in part because of the human rights violations the armed forces committed during the civil war, the military was removed from remote areas such as Quiche and Izabal at the war's end. Since that time, drug traffickers have taken advantage of the lack of a law enforcement presence in those areas to conduct their operations. Additionally, as Mexico increases its counter-narcotics efforts against them, Mexican drug cartels have expanded into Guatemala.

Guatemala is a major transit country for cocaine and heroin trafficked from South America to the United States, an activity increasingly linked to arms trafficking, according to the Department of State's 2014 U.S. International Narcotics Control Strategy Report. Money from narcotics trafficking and other illicit activities are laundered in Guatemala. Guatemala is a minor producer of opium poppy, and of increasing amounts of marijuana produced for domestic consumption.

President Proposes Revision of Drug Policies

As mentioned above, President Pérez Molina said that in response to drug-trafficking related violence alternatives to the current "war on drugs" needed to be considered, including legalizing the use and transport of certain drugs. (See "Illicit Drug Policy" above.)

Pérez Molina invited the other Central American presidents to discuss a major revision of counternarcotics policies and laws. Pérez Molina said he hoped to have a unified regional approach at the Summit of the Americas in April. But the presidents of El Salvador, Nicaragua, and Honduras apparently cancelled their attendance at the last minute without explanation, and then issued a statement on March 30 saying they oppose legalization of drugs and continue to support regional efforts to combat narcotics trafficking.[64] The three leaders present at the March 25 meeting, Ricardo Martinelli of Panama and Laura Chinchilla of Costa Rica, along with Pérez Molina, did not issue a policy declaration, but agreed to discuss several proposals further at a meeting of the Central American Integration System (SICA). The proposals include the decriminalization of drugs under certain conditions; creation of a regional penal court to handle drug trafficking cases; and compensation from drug-consuming nations—mainly the United States—for each shipment of drugs seized in Central America, and for the destruction of poppy and marijuana crops.

Pérez Molina has stated his government's position as fostering a global intergovernmental dialogue based on global regulations, "which means that consumption and production should be legalized but within certain limits and conditions." He also said that drug abuse, like alcoholism and tobacco use, "should be treated as public health problems, not criminal justice issues."[65]

---

[64] "Update:APNewsNow," *AP*, March 31, 2012.

[65] Otto Pérez Molina, "We Have to Find New Solutions to Latin America's Drugs Nightmare; Narcotics Should be Legally Available - in a Highly Regulated Market, Argues the President of Guatemala," *The Guardian*, April 7, 2012.

Colombian President Juan Manuel Santos had already put drug legalization and decriminalization on the agenda of the Summit of the Americas, which President Obama and a majority of other heads of state from the Americas attended in April 2012. Some of the other leaders criticized U.S. counternarcotics policy and urged a reconsideration of the so-called war on drugs. While President Obama listened to the arguments, he said he did not agree that decriminalization was a solution to the problem, and the summit ended without any joint declaration.[66] Presidents Obama and Pérez Molina met briefly at the summit.

In April 2014 Pérez Molina said that a government commission is studying a proposal to legalize marijuana and opium poppies production in Guatemala.[67] The commission is to release its recommendations in October. Guatemala will host an international conference on drug policy in September. Any proposal to unilaterally legalize marijuana and/or opium poppies is likely to meet strong opposition from the United States.

Pérez Molina continues to cooperate with the United States and other international partners on counter-narcotics efforts, and to pursue criminal cases against illicit drug trafficking. The Guatemalan government partners with the United States in security and counternarcotics programs through the Central American Regional Security Initiative (CARSI) (see "U.S. Relations With and Aid to Guatemala" below). The government has achieved some success, such as increasing the volume of drug seizures. The United States transferred the title and operational control of six UH-1H II helicopters to Guatemala's Ministry of Government in September 2013 after the government showed that it had the structure to sustain maintenance of the equipment. This nationalized Guatemala's aviation interdiction program, according to the State Department's 2014 *International Narcotics Control Strategy Report*. Guatemala also extradited a former President, Alfonso Portillo, to the United States in May 2013. Portillo had been indicted in 2009 in the United States on one count of conspiracy to commit money laundering in the United States. He pled guilty in March 2014 to bribery.

Nonetheless, according to the State Department's 2014 *International Narcotics Control Strategy Report*,

> While Guatemalan government agencies are maturing and gaining some momentum in the fight against drugs trafficking, they will not succeed in building durable and effective counter-narcotic enforcement organizations until the Guatemalan government fully implements its laws, provides adequate financial support, reforms its law enforcement culture, and professionalizes its judicial processes.[68]

Trade

Guatemala and the United States have significant trade relations. Since the Dominican Republic-Central America-United States Free Trade Agreement (CAFTA-DR) began to be implemented in 2006, bilateral trade has expanded greatly—much more so on the U.S. side. Supporters of CAFTA-DR point to reforms it spurred in transparency, customs administration, intellectual

---

[66] Frank Bajak and Vivian Sequera, "Cuba Split Leaves Summit Without Declaration," *The Miami Herald*, April 14, 2012.

[67] Economist Intelligence Unit, *Country Report: Guatemala*, May 2014, p. 22.

[68] U.S. Department of State, *International Narcotics Control Strategy Report*, http://www.state.gov/j/inl/rls/nrcrpt/2014/

property rights, and government regulation. Critics note that the commercial balance between the two countries previously favored Guatemala, and the balance has shifted in favor of the United States, with Guatemala registering its first trade deficit in a decade after CAFTA-DR was signed. According to U.S. Trade Representative (USTR) data, U.S. exports to Guatemala increased by 95% from 2005 (pre-CAFTA-DR) to 2013, while during the same period, Guatemalan exports to the United States increased by only 33%.[69] This is largely because Guatemalan exports to the United States received unilateral trade preferences before CAFTA-DR was implemented.

Total U.S.-Guatemalan trade in 2013 was $9.7 billion. The U.S. goods trade surplus with Guatemala was $1.4 billion. U.S. exports to Guatemala amounted to $5.5 billion. Oil, machinery, articles donated for relief and low value shipments, electrical machinery, and plastics parts accounted for the majority of U.S. exports. U.S. imports from Guatemala amounted to about $4.2 billion, with knit apparel, edible fruit and nuts, precious stones (gold), spices, coffee and tea, and woven apparel accounting for the majority. The United States is Guatemala's top trading partner and Guatemala is the United States' 53rd-largest trading partner.

The United States filed a case against Guatemala under CAFTA-DR in 2010, "the first labor case the United States has ever brought against a trade agreement partner," according to the office of the USTR.[70] In response to submissions filed by six Guatemalan unions and the AFL-CIO in 2008, the USTR conducted an investigation and found that "it appears that the Government of Guatemala is failing to meet its obligations under [CAFTA-DR] with respect to effective enforcement of Guatemalan labor laws related to the right of association, the right to organize and bargain collectively, and acceptable conditions of work." The USTR also expressed "grave" U.S. concerns regarding labor-related violence in Guatemala, "which is serious and apparently deteriorating." In April 2013 the two countries signed an 18-point Enforcement Plan outlining actions the country would take to strengthen enforcement of its labor laws.

In April 2014 U.S. Trade Representative Michael Froman announced that the case would not be terminated and would remain suspended for an additional four months. The USTR said that while Guatemala had taken some steps under the plan, "progress is not sufficient to close the case."[71] Among the steps Guatemala still needs to take are passage of legislation providing for an expedited process to sanction employers who violate labor laws, and implementation of a mechanism to ensure payment to workers when factories close suddenly.

Intercountry Adoption[72]

U.S. laws and policies concerning intercountry adoption are designed to ensure that all of the children put up for adoption are truly orphans, and have not been bought; kidnapped; or subjected to human trafficking, smuggling, or other illegal activities.

In FY2007, U.S. citizens adopted 4,726 children from Guatemala, more than from any other country except China (5,453). When the Hague Convention on Protection of Children and

---

[69] This and the data that follows is from: Office of the U.S. Trade Representative, *Guatemala: U.S.-Guatemala Trade Facts*, http://www.ustr.gov/countries-regions/americas/guatemala, April 29, 2014, accessed July 25, 2014.

[70] Quotes in this paragraph from: Office of the U.S. Trade Representative, *USTR Kirk Announces Labor Rights Trade Enforcement Case Against Guatemala*, Press release, Washington, PA, July 2010.

[7171] USTR, "United States Keeps in Place Labor Case against Guatemala," press release, April 2014.

[72] This section prepared by William Kandel, Analyst in Immigration Policy, Domestic Social Policy Division.

Cooperation in Respect of Intercountry Adoption (referred to hereafter as the Convention) went into effect in the United States that year, adoptions from Guatemala were suspended because Guatemala was not in compliance with the Convention's standards.

Since then, the only cases of adoptions by U.S. citizens of Guatemalan children that have been permitted are those that were already in-process in Guatemala on December 31, 2007.[73] There were over 3,000 such adoption cases pending at the time. In FY2013, the most recent year for which data are available, U.S. citizens adopted 23 children from Guatemala. As of July 30, 2014, there were 31 cases still pending.[74] The U.S. and Guatemalan governments have been working together to determine the status of these cases and to resolve the pending cases.[75] Not all of these cases are still active. Some have been closed and some may be cases where the prospective parents have abandoned their applications.

The United States is a signatory of the Convention. The goal of the Convention is to eliminate confusion and delays caused by differences among the laws and practices of different countries, and to ensure transparency in adoptions to prevent human trafficking, child stealing, or child selling.[76] As of June 1, 2014, the Convention had *entered into force* in 93 countries.[77] Countries can sign and ratify the Convention, but until the country has the laws and procedures in place to implement the Convention, the Convention cannot enter into force in the country.

The Convention entered into force in the United States on April 1, 2008, and governs intercountry adoptions between the United States and other Convention countries. Guatemala is party to the Convention,[78] but has not established regulations and procedures that meet Convention standards. As a result, the U.S. government is only processing petitions to allow an adopted child to immigrate to the United States for adoptions that were initiated in Guatemala prior to December 31, 2007,[79] because such adoptions can be completed under the non-Convention system.

---

[73] Department of State, *Intercountry Adoption, Guatemala,* updated March 2013, accessed by CRS on August 1, 2014, http://adoption.state.gov/country_information/country_specific_info.php?country-select=guatemala.

[74] Email correspondence from U.S. Department of State, Office of Children's Issues, Adoptions Division, July 30, 2014.

[75] Telephone conversation with U.S. Citizenship and Immigration Services, Office of Congressional Affairs, April 7, 2014.

[76] The Convention requires that: certain determinations, such as adoptability of the child, eligibility to immigrate, parent suitability and counseling be made before the adoption can proceed; every country establish a national government-level central authority to carry out certain functions that include cooperating with other central authorities, overseeing local implementation of the Convention, and providing access to information on adoption laws; a child's welfare be protected throughout the adoption process; certified adoptions be recognized in all other countries that are party to the Convention; and every country party to the Convention establish a national government-level process for uniform screening and authorization of adoption service providers.

[77] Hague Conference on Private International Law, *Status Table, 33: Convention of 29 May 1993 on Protection of Children and Co-operation in Respect of Intercountry Adoption*, Updated June 1, 2014, http://www.hcch.net/index_en.php?act=conventions.status&cid=69, accessed by CRS on August 1, 2014.

[78] Although the Guatemalan Constitutional Court ruled in 2004 that the country's signing of the Convention was unconstitutional, under international law, Guatemala is still party to the Convention and has been since March 1, 2003. Department of State, *"Frequently Asked Questions: Intercountry Adoptions and the Hague Convention: Guatemala,"* Oct. 12, 2008.

[79] Adoptions initiated in Guatemala prior to Dec. 31, 2007 are processed by the United States under non-Convention procedures. Since Guatemala refused to allow adoption from U.S. citizens between Dec. 31, 2007 and Apr. 1, 2008, all cases being processed were initiated in Guatemala prior to Dec. 31, 2007. Department of State, *Warning: Adoptions Initiated In Guatemala on or after April 1, 2008,* Apr. 1, 2008.

In September 2008, the Guatemalan National Adoption Council (CNA) announced it would not accept any new adoption cases to allow time to establish guidelines for accrediting adoption agencies and to focus on completing transition cases.[80] In August 2011, the CNA announced a plan, referred to as the *Acuerdo* (agreement), which provides a general processing framework for limited numbers of pending adoption cases already under CNA processing authority. In December 2011, the CNA confirmed details of the processing plan for such cases which are referred to as *acuerdo* cases. According to the Department of State (DOS), the CNA had referred 28 cases to the U.S. Embassy for final adoption processing as *acuerdo* cases between January 2012 and March 2013, and had identified others that it considered eligible to move through the *acuerdo* process.[81] The CNA does not charge fees for its adoption processing. This process does not apply to the earlier *notario* cases[82] pending with the Procuraduría General de la Nación (PGN).[83]

The United States will not approve new adoptions from Guatemala until Guatemala's adoption process complies with Convention standards, and there is no estimate of when that will be.[84]

Unaccompanied Children from Guatemala at the U.S. Border

The recent surge in the number of unaccompanied children being apprehended at the U.S. border, most of whom are from Central America, has caused much concern among Congress and the executive branch. From FY2009 to the first eight months of FY2014, the number of unaccompanied children from Guatemala apprehended by U.S. officials rose by 930%, from 1,115 to 12,670.[85]

Guatemalan Government Efforts to Address Root Causes of Migration

High levels of poverty, violence, and impunity for crimes, and the government's inability to provide many basic services, including security, are seen as major factors contributing to the migration of Guatemalans to the United States.[86] Despite social welfare programs implemented under the previous government of President Alvaro Colom, poverty increased between 2006 and 2011, from 51% to just under 54%.[87] Upon taking office in January 2012, President Pérez Molina

---

[80] More information about the CNA's September 2008 decision may be found on its website, http://www.cna.gob.gt.

[81] Department of State, *Intercountry Adoption, Guatemala,* updated March 2013, accessed by CRS on August 1, 2014, http://adoption.state.gov/country_information/country_specific_info.php?country-select=guatemala.

[82] Prior to the *Acuerdo,* all cases were processed by local lawyers and law professionals, or *notarios* and registered with the CNA. If such cases were registered with the CNA prior to the enactment of the Acuerdo, they could be processed under the prior notarial system. This process has been repeatedly criticized. See CRS Congressional Distribution Memorandum, *Current State of Intercountry Adoptions from Guatemala,* October 22, 2008, by Alison Siskin (available upon request).

[83] The PGN or Office of the Solicitor General of the Nation oversees the legality of notarial (*notario*) adoption cases. It conducts investigations of the orphan status for all children considered for adoption.

[84] Department of State, *Intercountry Adoption, Guatemala,* updated March 2013, accessed by CRS on August 1, 2014, http://adoption.state.gov/country_information/country_specific_info.php?country-select=guatemala.

[85] U.S. Border Patrol, "Unaccompanied Children (Age 0-17) Apprehensions, Fiscal Year 2008 through Fiscal Year 2012," February 4, 2013; and U.S. Customs and Border Protection, "Southwest Border Unaccompanied Alien Children," accessed July 2014.

[86] For more information, see CRS Report R43628, *Unaccompanied Alien Children: Potential Factors Contributing to Recent Immigration,* coordinated by William A. Kandel.

[87] World Bank, "Guatemala Overview," April 9, 2014.

---

established a Ministry of Social Development to implement social policy. (See "Social Policies" above.) Nonetheless, poverty remains high, with Guatemala having some of the lowest social indicators in the region, and having one of the most unequal distributions of wealth in the world. (See "Economic and Social Conditions" above.)

The Guatemalan government announced a Pact for Security, Justice and Peace in late 2012, a strategy involving all state institutions to improve governability, security, and protection from crime, violence and impunity.[88] While the government has made progress in strengthening some institutions, widespread corruption and impunity continue to limit the extent to which reforms can be carried out and maintained, and public confidence in Guatemalan institutions remains low.

The Pérez Molina Administration has been working with the Mexican government on border security and migration issues, including through a joint high level security group. The two countries, which share a 595-mile border, are also collaborating on development programs along both sides of the border, developing "green" crops to improve the standard of living there. The two also have agreed to build a gas pipeline from southern Mexico into Guatemala to increase their industrial competiveness.

While Pérez Molina has met with U.S. officials and other regional leaders to discuss strategies to address the current crisis, he has emphasized that efforts to create "a prosperous, modern, safe border with orderly migratory flows..." has to include the United States, and that "instead of putting up walls, obstacles and difficulties," there should be unity. [89] He has also asked that Guatemalan migrants be granted Temporary Protected Status until the United States passes comprehensive immigration reform.[90] Pérez Molina stood with Mexican President Enrique Pena Nieto on July 7, 2014, when the latter announced a Southern Border Security Campaign to protect the human rights of migrants passing from Guatemala and Belize through Mexico to the United States, and to strengthen border security. When Homeland Security Secretary Jeh Johnson met with President Pérez Molina in Guatemala on July 8, the two said they were seeking further ways to cooperate in combatting transnational crime and terrorism and strengthening borders.[91] First Lady Rosa Leal de Pérez launched a campaign called "Quedate," or "Stay Here," fully funded with Guatemalan resources, to encourage youth to stay in Guatemala rather than illegally emigrate to the United States.

Pérez Molina, along with the Presidents of El Salvador and Honduras, met with Members of Congress and President Obama and Vice President Joe Biden in Washington on July 24 and 25. President Pérez Molina suggested the need for a comprehensive regional program to promote security and economic and social development. He also reiterated his request for TPS for Guatemalans until U.S. migration reform is enacted, to which the United States has not responded. President Obama said the United States has compassion for the children, but reiterated that those who do not have proper claims to remain here will be returned to their country of origin.[92] He also mentioned a pilot program the Administration is considering for Honduras which

---

[88] Gobierno de Guatemala, Ministerio de Gobernación, http://www.mingob.gob.gt/index.php?option=com_k2&view=item&layout=item&id=381&Itemid=563, accessed July 9, 2014.

[89] Francisco Reséndiz Enviado, "Va Plan de ayuda a ninos migrantes," *El Universal*, July 8, 2014.

[90] "Mexican and Guatemalan Leaders Tackle Child Migrant Crisis," *Latin News Daily Report*, July 8, 2014.

[91] Gobierno de Guatemala, Ministerio de Gobernación, "Afirman Lucha contra el Crimen Transnacional y Terrorismo," July 8, 2014.

[92] Jim Kuhnenn and Erica Werner, "Obama Prods GOP on Border Issue, Cites Progress," AP, July 26, 2014.

would screen youths while still in their country to determine whether they qualify for refugee status. Although the program could possibly be extended to include Guatemala and El Salvador, the President said only a small number of people would qualify. President Obama also said the United States was committed to working in partnership with the three countries "to find ways in which we can come up with more aggressive action plans to improve security and development and governance in these countries."[93]

On July 8, President Obama submitted to Congress a $3.7 billion supplemental request to address increased migration from Central America. The majority of funding would go toward border security and enforcement efforts. Just under 8% of the funding would be allotted for "the repatriation and reintegration of migrants to countries in Central America and to address the root causes of migration from these countries."

Support Programs in Guatemala for Returned Migrants. In response to the dramatic increase in the number of Guatemalans removed from the United States, and related problems or consequences, the Guatemalan and U.S. governments have initiated programs to support returning migrants during the past few years. In 2004, the Guatemalan government estimated that 7,029 Guatemalans, including 200 children, were deported from the United States. By 2012, that number had increased by almost 600% to 40,647, including 586 children.[94] In FY2013, the Department of Homeland Security (DHS) removed 47,215 Guatemalans from the United States. About 33% of those had criminal records.[95] The data did not indicate how many of those removed in 2013 were minors. In FY2011, the most recent year for which U.S. data for removal of unaccompanied minors is available, DHS removed 458 unaccompanied children originally from Guatemala.[96] Recognizing the obstacles faced by repatriated people, and their possible contribution to social instability if left unsupported, the U.S. Agency for International Development (USAID) launched the now ended two-year Guatemalan Repatriates Project with IOM in 2011.[97]

---

[93] The White House, "Remarks by President Obama After Meeting with Central American Presidents," July 25, 2014.

[94] These migration figures are from the Guatemalan government as cited in: International Organization for Migration (IOM): *Migration initiatives Appeal 2010*, 2010, p 72 (2004 data); "Migracion en Guatemala (Cifras)," August 31, 2013, pp.1-2.They may not correspond exactly with figures from the Department of Homeland Security (DHS), Office of Immigration Statistics, *2004 Yearbook of Immigration Statistics.* DHS calculates removals by fiscal year. In FY2004, DHS removed 8,235 Guatemalans. In FY2012, DHS removed 38,677 Guatemalans. DHS, Office of Immigration Statistics, *2012 Yearbook of Immigration Statistics.*

[95] DHS, Bureau of Immigration and Customs Enforcement, *2013 Removals by Departed to Country.*

[96] U.S. Department of Health and Human Services (HHS), *Report to Congress on the Provision of P.L. 110-457 Regarding Repatriation of Unaccompanied Alien Children and U.S. Government Efforts to Protect Them from Human Trafficking,* January 16, 2013, p. 2.

[97] IOM, "Press Conference on the Guatemalan Repatriates Project," June 3, 2011.

Guatemalan Repatriates Project

Overview

The Guatemalan Repatriates Project expanded the services provided to deportees arriving both by air from the United States at the Guatemalan Air Force Base in Guatemala City and by land from Mexico through San Marcos. Shelters are at both locations. Immediate assistance included an initial needs assessment, the provision of hygiene kits, psychosocial support, legal advice, and transportation to communities of origin. Reintegration services included vocational training and job placement programs in the capital.

The Guatemalan Repatriates Project proved less effective at providing longer-term support for the reintegration of repatriated Guatemalans than at providing short-term aid. Of the 88,153 Guatemalans assisted by the Guatemalan Repatriates Project from June 2011 to July 2013, only 4,457 were housed at the two shelters. Only about 3,000 of those Guatemalans received comprehensive social and/or economic reintegration assistance in Guatemala City. Although most were from poor rural areas, 184 Guatemalans received such services elsewhere in Guatemala. The Repatriates Project worked with companies willing to hire returnees; 397 Guatemalans were referred to that network, and just 55 were hired during that two-year period.

Outcomes and Government Action

Now that the USAID- funded pilot project has ended, the Guatemalan government is providing much of the same immediate assistance, but the project's reintegration services are no longer being provided. The Guatemalan government has greatly expanded its presence at the reception center at the Guatemalan Air Force Base. Numerous ministries and agencies are present to help the 90 to 135 repatriates arriving on two to three flights daily. Reception services now provided or facilitated by the government include motivational welcome talks, refreshments, free phone calls, on-site banking for changing money, and psychological care. Immigration officials help process returnees; National Registry officials begin the process of getting returnees a national identification card; the Foreign Affairs Ministry explains available services and offers help such as buying transportation tickets to remote areas; and the Health Ministry has a clinical office on the premises. The U.S. and Guatemalan governments see the reception center as a model for the region in providing services upon reentry.

Since 2012, unaccompanied minors being repatriated have been processed in an area separate from adults. The Guatemalan government and several NGOs offer support to unaccompanied minors deported to Guatemala. For example, the Attorney General's office takes custody of children until family or other guardians can be found. The Ministry for Social Well-Being coordinates a shelter for children in Guatemala City which provides psychosocial, legal, education and health assistance to human trafficking victims. From June 2011 to July 2013, 124 minors were assisted at the shelter.[98] The NGOs Global Fund for Children (GFC) and Kids in Need of Defense (KIND) work with four Guatemalan nonprofit community-based organizations to provide services through the Guatemalan Child Return and Reintegration Project. Services include pro bono legal help during the removal process in the United States, and upon return to Guatemala, temporary shelter, family reunification assistance, psychological services, education, job training, employment assistance, and workshops to support social reintegration. GFC and KIND say they will take the best practices learned from the pilot project and promote similar projects elsewhere in the region.[99]

Guatemala established the National Council for Attention to Migrants (Consejo Nacional de Atencion al Migrante, CONAMIGUA) several years ago, which initially provided services to Guatemalan migrants in the United States, and kept records on immigrants in Guatemala and repatriates to Guatemala. In 2013, about 20% of its budget was dedicated to new reintegration

---

[98] Ibid.

[99] Kids in Need of Defense, http://www.supportkind.org/en/kind-in-action/guatemala-return-and-reintegration-project, accessed May 12, 2014.

services for repatriates.[100] IOM has also provided capacity-building for government officials, focusing on the prevention of human trafficking, the protection of victims, and the prosecution of perpetrators.

When Vice President Biden visited Guatemala in June 2014 to speak with President Pérez Molina and leaders from El Salvador and Honduras, he promised an additional $9.6 million to help those countries receive and reintegrate their repatriated citizens. In Guatemala, USAID will use some of those funds to work with IOM to provide services and goods such as those given earlier through the Guatemalan Repatriates Project—food, water, temporary housing, transportation to home communities, medical and psychosocial support. They will also give support to Guatemalan officials for processing returned citizens, and train officials on working with returned children and their families. Vice President also announced $40 million for a new five-year USAID program in Guatemala to improve citizen security, including reducing risk factors for youth involvement in gangs; and $161.5 million for CARSI programs to address some of the root causes of migration, such as prevention activities for at-risk youth, and programs to strengthen the rule of law.

On July 8, President Barack Obama submitted to Congress a $3.7 billion supplemental request to address increased migration from Central America. The majority of funding would go toward border security and enforcement efforts. Just under 8% of the funding, or $295 million, would be allotted for "the repatriation and reintegration of migrants to countries in Central America and to address the root causes of migration from these countries." Of that amount, USAID would be allotted $25 million to expand community-based programs to reduce youth crime and violence.

Author Contact Information

Maureen Taft-Morales
Specialist in Latin American Affairs
mtmorales@crs.loc.gov, 7-7659

---

[100] Lee Hopkins, "Making Guatemala 'Home' Again: Service Approaches for Sustainable Reintegration of Repatriates in Guatemala," Columbia University Partnership for International Development Online Journal, February 9, 2014, p. 2.